My P

Go Wild for Word

The Quick Guide for Microsoft Word

Live, Love, Learn

This book is dedicated to my family and friends, near and far.
Without your support these pages couldn't be written.

A tribute to my Dad.

The "My Parents" computer guide books
help to raise funds for cancer research and patient care.
Find a cure.

Published by KLMK Enterprises
A small publishing house that knows no boundaries.

www.MyParentsFirst.com

ISBN 978-0-9732728-88
Printed in Winnipeg, MB, Canada 2011
© All Rights Reserved. Louise Latremouille

The My Parents Computer Guides

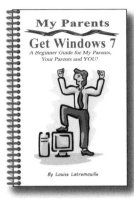

Enjoy these other titles from Louise Latremouille:

◊ My Parents Get Windows 7
◊ My Parents First Computer Guide
◊ My Parents Computer Guide, Beyond the Basics
◊ My Parents Went Mac!

The *My Parents* computer guides are written in plain everyday language with a conversational tone. Reading them is like having a patient teacher gently guiding you along.

The quick, step-by-step instructions will have you enjoying your computer in no time at all. The guides feature large print and simple graphics. The spiral binding makes them easy to fold open for a handy reference beside your computer. They are simply the best beginner books around!

About the author:

Louise's first book, *My Parents First Computer and Internet Guide*, actually grew out of the notes she wrote to her own parents while her dad was battling lung cancer. Her parents inherited a computer and were struggling to learn how to use "that darn thing".

It was her dad who saw the potential of her notes and suggested she organize them into a book. He lost his battle with cancer, but continues to inspire her every day. Live, love and learn with joy.

In hope for a cure, sales from her books help support cancer research and patient care.

About Microsoft Word

Microsoft's Word© has a lot going for it. You'll be surprised how easy it is to use, whether you're typing simple notes or making fancy documents.

Microsoft Word had a major revamp in 2007.

In earlier versions of Word you found the commands in a Menu Bar along the top of its window. The Menu Bar showed headings: File, Edit, View, etc. You clicked on a heading to see the commands listed below.

In 2007, Microsoft changed Word and in 2010 they tweaked it again! Now the commands and tools are shown as icons, grouped together along a Ribbon.

If you are using a computer with Windows XP, or any operating system prior to Windows 7, you probably have an older version of Word installed.

If you are using an earlier version of Microsoft Word, please pick up *My Parents First Computer and Internet Guide.* It will give you all the help you need! Then if you want to do more, pick up *My Parents Computer Guide; Beyond the Basics.*

This book is for
Microsoft Word 2007 or 2010,
on a computer with Windows 7.

Thank you to Microsoft, who gives us permission
to use their material and some images so we can help you on your way!

My Parents Go Wild for Word

Go Wild for Word

Get Started	1
The Tour Guide	21
Working with Tables	56
Working with Pictures	62
The Command Index	67

Enjoy learning how to use Microsoft Word. ☺

Be sure to write down your own notes and bright ideas.

Ready? Let's go!

Get Started

Microsoft Word is one of the most popular word processing programs in the world.

It's taught in schools, used in offices and is a super program to have in your home computer.

Soon you'll learn about the many wonderful things Word can do. First though, let's *get started* with the basics...

Get Started

Opening Word	1
Create a Document	2
Save a Document	4
Your Library	5
Quick Access Toolbar	7
Close Documents	8
Moving Windows	9
Open Documents	10
Printing	11
Default Font	15
Word Options	16
Status Bar	19
Tabs, Ribbons & Groups	20

Opening Word

Here's a couple ways to open Word, or any other program for that matter, with Windows 7.

1. **Through the Start menu.**
   a. Left click on the Start button.
   b. Then, right above where it says *Search programs and files*, type in "Word".
   c. You'll see *Microsoft Office Word* appear in the Start menu column above.
   d. To open Word, move your mouse up and left-click on *Microsoft Office Word*.

2. **Create a shortcut.**
   - Follow the steps above, but **instead of left-clicking** on Microsoft Word, **right-click over it** to open a mouse menu.
   - The mouse menu will look something like this.
   - To make the shortcut, slide your mouse over and left-click on either:

     Pin to Taskbar, or

     Pin to Start menu

   If you chose *Pin to Taskbar*, you'll place an icon for Word in your Taskbar.

   The Taskbar is the bar that runs all along at the bottom of your screen. The Start button sits on the left side of it.

   If you chose *Pin to Start Menu*, the next time you click on the Start button you'll see it listed in the column right above. *You won't have to search for it.* Just slide your mouse up and left-click on Word to open the program!

Open
Troubleshoot Compatibility
Pin to Taskbar
Pin to Start Menu
Send to
Delete
Properties

Pinning your favorite programs

to either the Taskbar or the Start Menu

is a great way to quickly access them in the future.

Create and Save

It's easier to learn by doing, so... open Word and let's go!

Click through this path to open Word:

Start > Microsoft Office Word.

If you created a shortcut for Word along your taskbar, click on the shortcut!

When you first open Word, it will open on the Home tab
with a new letter-size page, ready for you to type in.

NOTE
In the book, if I just say "CLICK", I want you to LEFT-CLICK.

When you move your mouse around the screen and left-click, the cursor will instantly arrive at that spot. The left-click also executes commands.

A mouse usually comes programmed for right-handed people, where the right-click will open a mouse-menu of commands and the left-click will execute commands.

If you're left-handed and want to personalize your mouse, click through this path and choose your mouse options:

Start > Control Panel > Personalize > Mouse Options

Create and Save

Let's create a little document and save it.
You can use this document throughout the book for something to practice on when we learn new things.

Creating a document
Just by opening Word, you have begun creating a document.

◊   Look to the top of your screen and you'll see Document1. That's the default name that Word gives the first open document of any session.

◊   If you opened a second new document it would be called Document2...

◊   When you save a document you can name it almost anything you like. After it is saved, it becomes a file in your computer.

Click your mouse into the main body of the document and type this familiar little ditty: (Hit the Return/Enter key to go to the next line.)

**Row, row, row your boat,
Gently down the stream.
Merrily, merrily, merrily, merrily,
Life is but a dream.**

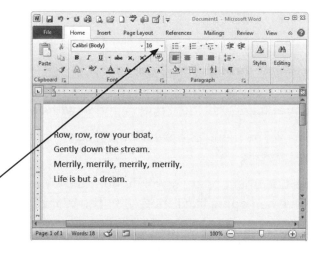

The typing on your document will probably look a little smaller than what I show here. I've changed the size of my type (font) to 16, so you can see it easier in this graphic.

If you want to change the size of the font on yours, click on the little arrow that I'm pointing to. Then, move your mouse down the list and click on any of the numbers to choose a size. Or, you can just type a new number in the font size box!

Create and Save

Saving a document.

If you are using Word 2007, you will click on the Office logo to open its File menu. In 2010, the Office logo was replaced with a File tab.

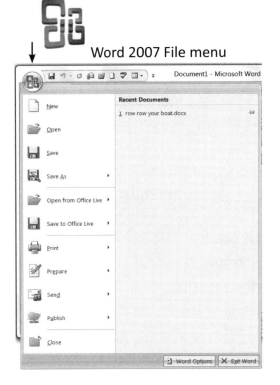

Word 2007 File menu

Word 2010 File menu

Here's how to save a document through the File menu.

1. **Click on File** (or the Office logo) and you'll open a menu with *Save* in it.
   ◊ When you click on File, its menu *and window* will open, covering up the document you are working on.
   ◊ If you don't have a document open, it will default to showing a list of recent documents you have had open; like I show with the Word 2007 File menu.
   ◊ If you have started to create a document the File menu defaults to *Info*; like I show with the Word 2010 File menu. It shows information about the document you have open.

2. **Slide your mouse and click on Save or Save As**, to open the *Save As* window.
   ◊ The File menu closes and the Save As window opens.

4

Create and Save

◊ Now you can see your document window again, behind the Save As window.

◊ Have a look in the left column. This is where you are going to save your file, in your Documents folder.

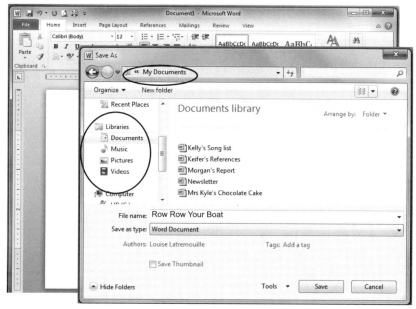

Over, to step 3 →

Tip

On the left side of this window, you'll see your **Library**. The Library holds the folders that will help you, and your computer, stay organized. The folders are:

Documents, Music, Pictures and Videos.

Before you save a file, think about what type of file you're saving.
Then, save it in the right spot!

Documents → Documents folder
Music → Music folder
Pictures → Pictures folder
Videos → Videos folder

Create and Save

Saving a document...

3. **Click on the Documents folder, under Libraries,** to tell your computer that's where you want to save the file.
   ◊ *Notice that it says "My Documents" or, just "Documents" in the top header. That top little window will always tell you what folder you are in.*

4. **Name your document.** Type *Row Row Your Boat* in the box beside *File name*.
   ◊ Notice that it is saving the *file type* as a Word Document. Word will put a .doc or .docx extension at the end of its name.

5. **Click on Save.** There — now you have created a file!

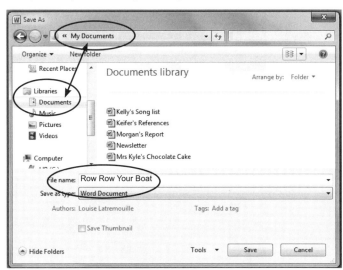

Here's a re-cap of how to Save a Document...

1. Click on File > Save > Documents folder
2. Click in the File name box and name your document
3. Click on Save.

Or we could just say:

File > Save > Documents folder > Name it > Save it

Tip: **.doc** vs **.docx**
In 2007 the default format for saving Word files became .docx
Before that, the default format was .doc

Older versions of Word need to download the free Office Compatibility Pack from Microsoft to be able to read .docx type files. In newer versions of Word, you can actually still save a document as a .doc type file. In the Save As window, look to where it says "Save as type". Click on the arrow that's on the right of that space to see all the different types of files you can save a document as!

Quick Access Toolbar

The little row at the top of the window is the **Quick Access Toolbar.** You might want to customize it with your favourite commands. It's easy to do — here's how:

1. Click on the little drop-down arrow that's on the right side of the Quick Access icons to open this little menu.

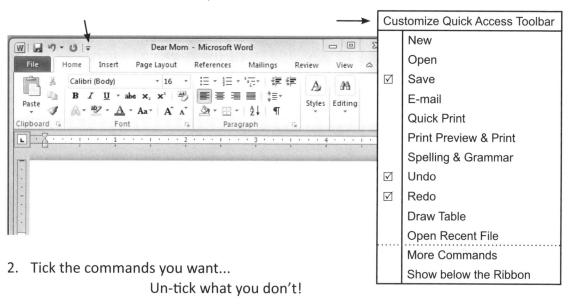

2. Tick the commands you want...
   Un-tick what you don't!

Nice, to customize your ride...
You can change it any time you want.

Did you notice this icon  **along the Quick Access Toolbar?**

This is the Save icon, and clicking on it is another way to save a document!

◊ If you have not yet saved the document you are working on, clicking on this icon will open the Save *As window*.

◊ **After** a document is saved, clicking on the Save icon will update any changes you've made to the file.

◊ If ever you want to save a file or document with a different name, use the *Save As* command through the File menu.

7

Close Documents

Now that you've saved a document, let's close it.

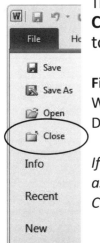

This is one way to close a document.
Click on File (or the Office logo in Word 07),
to open the File menu.

File > Close
When you click on Close, you will close the document you have open.
Documents are saved as files in your computer.

If you've done any work on a document since you last saved it, Word will ask you if you want to save your changes before closing it.
Click on Yes if you do want to save your changes, No if you don't.

File > Exit
In Word 2010, Exit is on the bottom of the File menu. Click on Exit and not only will you close the document, you will also exit and close Word.

Learn about another way to exit a document or program on the next page!

In Word 2007 you will see

Exit Word in the bottom corner of

the File menu,

beside Word Options.

8

Moving and Sizing a Window

You'll see these three boxes on most windows, in any program.

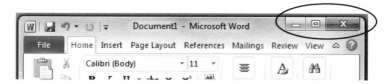

Here's what they do:

◊ You can change the size of the window by clicking in the middle of these three boxes. There's only two sizes this box creates, either a full-screen or a mid-sized screen.

◊ Click on the little line in the left box to minimize that window into the taskbar. To re-open it, all you have to do is click on its icon in the taskbar.

◊ Click on the "X" to exit or close the document and/or program. Clicking on this X is the other way to close a document!

Here's how to manually change the size of your window:

1. Move your mouse to the edge of Word's window; either side, top or bottom. (Not the edge of the page; the edge of *Word's* window.) You'll see a double arrow appear. ⟷
   Hold down the left-click when you see it.

2. While holding down the left click, slide your mouse to enlarge or shrink the window.

    ◊ *Notice when you shrink the width of the window that fewer tools show on the Ribbon.*

Here's how to move a window around on your screen:

1. Hold the left click down on the header bar, by where it says Document 1, and move your mouse.

2. Let go of the click when the window is where you want it.

Drag and drop, that's it!

9

Open Documents

If you exited Word, open Word again... Then, to open a Word document, click through: File > Open (with Word 07: Office Logo > Open). You will open a window like this one.

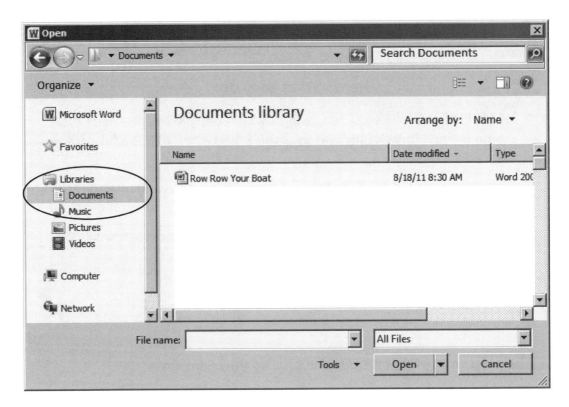

◊ Make sure "Documents", under Library in the left sidebar, is highlighted to see all the files that are saved within the Documents folder. If it's not, click on Documents to select it.

◊ Click your mouse on the name of your file, in this case *Row Row Your Boat*.

 ◊ If you click once on a file's name, it will appear in the File name box below. Then, click on Open to open it.

 ◊ If you double click on a file name, it will open automatically.

Look at your Library to see what folder you are looking in...

Printing with Word 2010

If you have customized your Quick Access Toolbar to include the *Print Preview and Print* icon, you can click there to open the Print Window.

If you don't have the Print icon on your Quick Access Toolbar, click
File > Print to open the Print window.
This is the window that opens with Word 2010.
If you are using Word 07, please turn the page to learn about your Print window.

The middle column in the 2010 Print Window shows all your printing options.

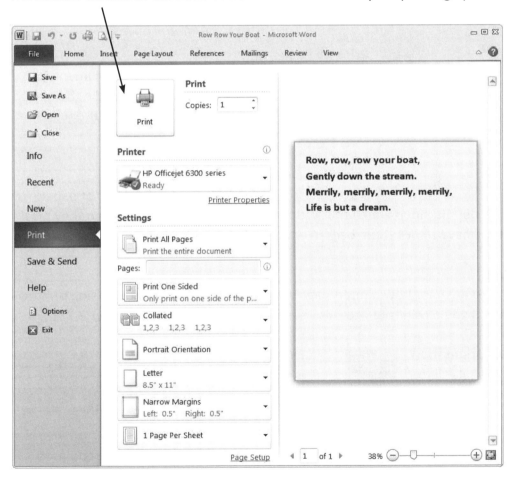

When you have selected the options you want, **click on the big Print button,** seen at the top of the middle column, to print the document.

The printing options available to you will depend on the printer you have. I'll tell you about some of the more common options on the next page!

11

Printing Options

Printing Options

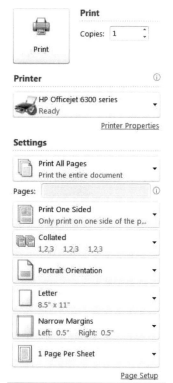

Set the number of copies to print
You can adjust how many copies you want to print by using the little arrows or just by typing in the number of copies you want in the box beside where it says Copies.

Printer
Your printer should be reflected here, with a green check mark on it, status Ready. If it's not, click on the drop-down arrow to see if your printer's listed. If you don't see yours listed, better check and see if it's connected to your computer—and turned on!

Print All Pages, or…
You can choose to print all or part of a document, just click on the little arrow to see your options. I like the option to print "the selection". Highlight a bit of your document, then choose this option to print just that bit.

Print One Sided, or…
You can also print on both sides of a sheet of paper. When you print double-sided watch that the sheets don't get mixed up when they print out, as you will have to put them back in your printers' feeder to print on the second side.

Collated
Use this to organize how a multi-page document is organized while being printed. For instance, it could print out like this: pages 1,1,1/2,2,2/3,3,3 or 1,2,3/1,2,3/1,2,3 .

Portrait Orientation
is like a regular letter.

Landscape Orientation
is wider than it is tall.

Letter…
This is where you set **what size of paper you're printing on**. A4 is the common letter size outside Canada and the USA. You'll see lots of paper sizes here, as well as envelope sizes!

Margins
You can adjust the margins of your document here. You will also find tools to adjust page margins under the Page Layout tab.

Printing with Word 07

Printing a document with Word 07
1. Click on the Office icon to open the File menu.
2. Click on Print to open the Print window.

Good printing options to know about are...

◊ **Page Range:** Do you want to print all of your document, just the current page or maybe just a range of pages?

◊ **Copies:** Adjust how many copies you want to print here.

◊ **Properties:** This is the button right beside your printer's name. Click on this button to open a window where you can adjust the quality of printing. For instance, you might like to use Fast Draft for everyday printing, and Photo Quality for pictures. As you can imagine, one uses a lot more ink than the other!

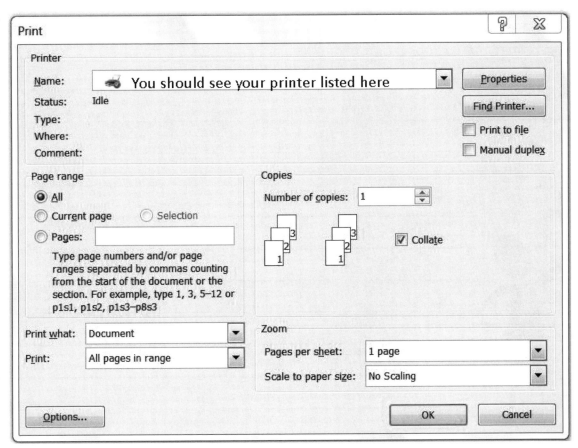

Bright Ideas

Default Font

When Word opens, it's on the Home tab with a blank page ready for you to type on. The style and size of font is all preset. Here you see the font is Calibri (Body) at size 11. You will find most of the choices to personalize Word in Options, under the File menu.
Setting the default font though, is part of the Font Group. Here's how to change it:

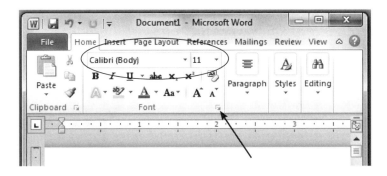

1. In the above picture, see the little arrow along the bottom of the font group? Click on yours, to open the Font options window.

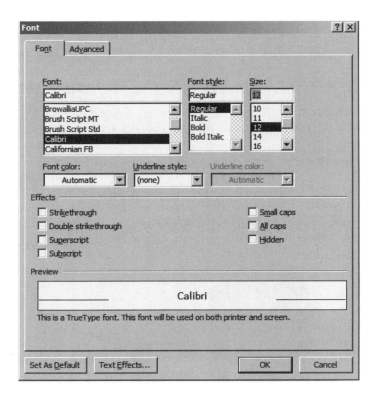

2. In the Font Options window you can choose any font, style and size you want.
3. Once you have chosen the font you want, click on the "Set As Default" button at the bottom of the Font Options window. Next time Word opens it will be on this font!

That's it! You can change it any time you want.

File > Options

Personalize Word with Options.
File > Options, that is.

Even though you might not want to tinker with your options right away, it's nice to know what they are. That way in the future, when you're thinking... "Oh I wish Word worked like this or did that", you'll remember, "Hey — it can!"

The Office logo was replaced with the File tab in Word 2010.

If you are using Word 2007,
in the Tour Guide and Command Index,
when I say to click on File,
you will click on the Office logo instead.

File > Options

Click on File > Options, to open the Options window.

You'll see the Option headings in the left sidebar.
Click on a heading to see what's there. *With Word 07, General is called Popular.*

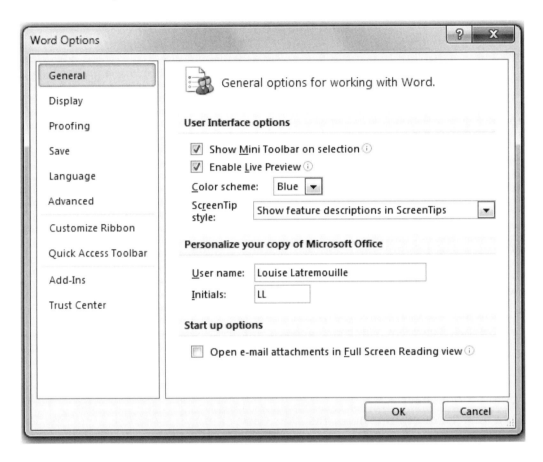

- ◊ Tick the box beside an option to enable it, un-tick it to leave it off.
- ◊ Click on little drop-down arrows to see what choices you have.
- ◊ Fill in your name in the User Name box and put in your initials.

I'm not going to go over the obvious things here, but you might wonder what a few things are. Turn over the page to see what's what. For instance:

File > Options > General > Show Mini Toolbar on selection *(General is Popular in 07)*
If this is enabled, when you highlight a bit of text, you'll see a small box with a few basic formatting tools appear faintly right beside your cursor. If you slide your mouse over top of the box, you can use the tools. Why use this? So you won't have to move your mouse *all the way* up to the Ribbon to change basic formatting.

File > Options

File > Options > General > Enable Live Preview
If *Live Preview* is enabled, just by hovering over a command, you can see what different formatting options look like on your document. Live Preview is especially handy when you are working with pictures.

File > Options > Display
You'll find a few options here to define what hidden characters are displayed, as-well-as the option to say whether or not pictures are included when you print a document!

File > Options > Proofing
This is where you'll find the Auto-correct, Spell Check and Grammar options.

File > Options > Save
You can tell Word how often to automatically save/update your documents here. Auto-Save is a very good thing! You can also change the default folder that documents are saved into here. The Documents folder is the default folder documents are saved in.

File > Options > Language
Is U.S. English your language of choice? Canadian English, Spanish, French?... Word is available in many languages. This is where you set up the default language you want to work in.

File > Options > Advanced
You'll find a long list of options here, including basic editing options like Cut, Copy, Paste and Display options. You have to use the scroll bar on the right side of the window to see all the options listed here.

File > Options > Customize Ribbon
If you find the ribbon is overwhelming, with too many tools showing, you can come here and choose what tabs, tools and commands you would like to see displayed. You can customize the ribbon to show what you want.

File > Options > Add-Ins and the Trust Center
Don't mess with Add-Ins unless you know what you're doing. Add-Ins generally help Word work better.
As for the Trust Center, that's where you will find Microsoft Word's privacy statements.

Status Bar

There is good information lurking at the bottom of Word's window...

The bar at the bottom of the window is called the Status Bar.
You can customize what the Status Bar shows! Here's how:

1. Right-click your mouse anywhere along the status bar to open a menu with lots of options.
2. Just like you customized the Quick Access Toolbar...
   Tick the options you want, un-tick what you don't!

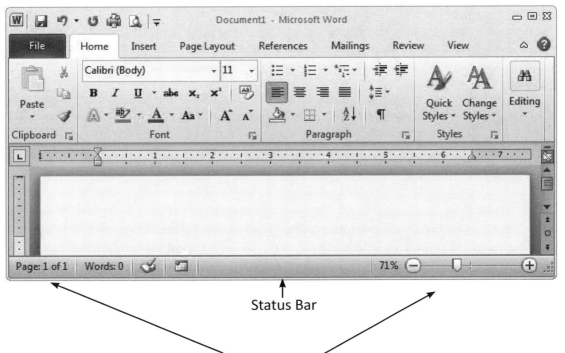

Status Bar

I like having Page and the Zoom Slider showing.
The Zoom Slider is very handy for those with poor vision.
And Page is great for knowing if I've kept my work to one page.
*I'm often frustrated when I think I'm printing one page
and two pages print out...*

When you hit the return key to go down to the next line, you create a "hidden character" on your page that looks like this ¶. You don't see it unless you choose to see hidden characters.

Find the tool to show/hide hidden characters in the Paragraph Group, under the Home tab. Seeing hidden characters all the time is a little wacky. Most of us find it's easier to leave them hidden.

19

Tabs, Ribbon and Groups

What's what...

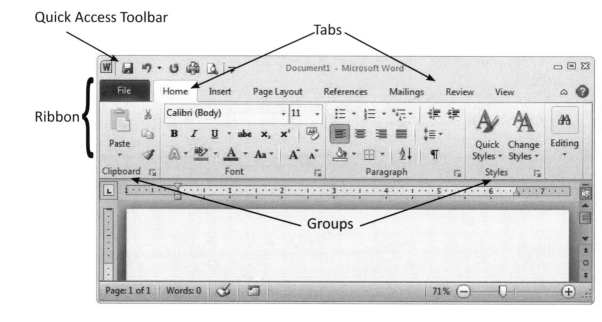

The Ribbon
The Ribbon shows the tools and commands. Some commands are spelled out, but most are represented by an icon. Find related commands under the different Tabs.

The Tabs
The headings are called Tabs: File, Home, Insert, etc... Click on a Tab to see the commands that are associated with that heading. Commands that work together are organized in Groups.

The Groups
Commands and tools that go together are grouped together. You will see the name of each Group near the bottom of the ribbon. Clipboard, Font, Paragraph, etc...

Next, follow The Tour Guide
to learn about the commands in Word.

You will be amazed at how much Word can do
and, how fast you can learn how to use it!

The Tour Guide

Follow along with the Tour Guide on your computer.
Learn what commands are where, and how to use them.
Use the file we created, or another one of your own,
to try out the commands.

The Tour Guide is organized by each tab, from left to right.
The commands under each tab are organized by Groups, *except the File tab*.
The commands under the File tab (Or under the Office logo with Word 07) are listed as a Menu.

Here's how to use the Tour Guide:

Open *Microsoft Word* on your computer.

1. Click on **the Tab** that's featured in the row you are looking at in the Tour Guide.

2. Now, look for **the Group** that's in that row. The Groups are organized left to right as they are laid out in Word. *The File menu is the exception to this rule...*

3. T**he Commands** in each Group are organized left to right, top to bottom. Look at and click on the command that's shown on that row.

4. Read about what the command is for and how to use it. Try it out. *Go wild!*

Here is a sample of one row in the Tour Guide...

Tab	Group	Command	Icon	Use
Home	Clipboard	**Paste**		Use this to Paste an image or text **after** you have "copied" it. The keyboard shortcut for Paste is Ctrl + V

Take The Tour and Learn your way around!

21

The Tour Guide

I know I've said it before, but to help with any confusion... here it is again.
The Office logo was replaced with the File tab in Word 2010.
If you are using Word 2007, in the Tour Guide and Command Index, when I say to click on File, you will click on the Office logo instead.

The Tour Guide is organized by each Tab, from left to right.
The commands under each Tab are organized by Groups.

The File tab is the exception to the rule.
The commands under the File tab are listed as a menu.
(Or under the Office logo with Word 07.)

It's time to start! Open Word, click on File, and follow along.

The Tour Guide

TAB	GROUP	COMMAND	ICON	USE
File	*With Word 2007, click on the Office icon*	**Save or Save As**		**File > Save** This is where you find the tools to save a document. If you click on either Save or Save As, you'll open the Save As window. More on saving documents starting on page 4.
File	*With Word 2010, click on File*	**Open**		**File > Open** Click through File > Open to open a window where you can search for a saved document. More on Opening documents on page 10.
File		**Close**		**File > Close** Use the Close command to close a document, but leave Word open. More on closing a document on page 8.
File		**Info**		**File > Info** If you have a document open when you click on File, it automatically defaults to opening on Info, showing you basic information about that document. The Info screen covers up the page you are working on. The page you are working on is still there, just behind this information. This is also where you can set up ***document protection***, *set up a* ***password*** *or prepare it for* ***sharing***.
File		**Recent**		**File > Recent** Click on Recent to see a list of all the saved files you've recently had open, with the most recent at the top of the list. Just slide your mouse over and click on the name of the file you want to open.

23

The Tour Guide

TAB	GROUP	COMMAND	ICON	USE
File	*With Word 2007, click on the Office icon*	New		**File > New** Click on New to see all the different types of documents Word can create. From a plain blank page to fancy documents like resumes, faxes, cards, agendas, calendars... So many choices!
File		Print		**File > Print** Click through this path to open the print window. To learn more about how to print go to page 11.
File	*With Word 2010, click on File*	Save & Send		**File > Save & Send** These tools can help you to save your document in a variety of formats suitable for emailing, posting on a blog, putting on a website or sending to another computer in your network.
File		Help		**File > Help** Click on the question mark icon to open Microsoft's *online* help pages. If you're not on the internet, Help isn't much help... This is also where you get Word to check for online updates.
File		Options		**File > Options** Find the *Options* here to personalize and customize Word. Learn more about these Options starting on page 16.
File		Exit		**File > Exit** Click on Exit and you will exit and close Word and the document you are working on. With Word 07, find *Exit Word* on a button on the bottom right corner of the window.

24

The Tour Guide

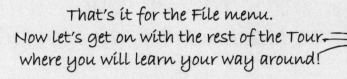

That's it for the File menu.
Now let's get on with the rest of the Tour,
where you will learn your way around!

Tip:
With most commands,
click on them once to activate them,
click on them again to turn them off.

Bright Ideas...

The Tour Guide

*Follow The Tour Guide,
row by row,
to learn your way around.*

Ready?
Let's walk through this first row together.

1. **Under the TAB heading,** in this first row, you'll see Home.
   ◊ Click on the Home tab in Word on your computer.

2. **Under the GROUP heading**, find where it says Clipboard.
   ◊ *Clipboard* is the first *Group* on the left side of the Ribbon.

3. **Under the COMMAND heading**, find Paste.
   ◊ Until you copy something, Paste will be grayed out. When a command is grayed out it means you have not done what it takes to make that command work. In this case, you haven't copied anything yet to paste! **Copy is the next command. When you are there, please copy something, move your cursor to another location on your document and click on Paste to get the hang of it. It's a very useful, cool tool!

4. **Under the ICON heading**, see the icon (little picture) that represents Paste.

5. **Under the USE heading,** read what that command is and how to use it.

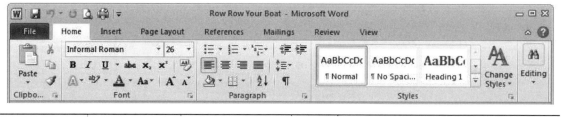

TAB	GROUP	COMMAND	ICON	USE
Home	Clipboard	**Paste**		Use this to Paste an image or text *after* you have "copied" it. The keyboard shortcut for Paste is Ctrl + V

Keep going!

26

The Tour Guide

TAB	GROUP	COMMAND	ICON	USE
Home	Clipboard	**Copy**		Highlight text or an image then click on Copy to copy it. Then, click your cursor to where you want to put it and click on Paste! Ta da! The keyboard shortcut for Copy is Ctrl + C
Home	Clipboard	**Cut**		Highlight an image or text, click on Cut to "cut" it out of the document, ready to *Paste* somewhere else.
Home	Clipboard	**Format Painter**		Highlight a typing format you like, then click on the Format Painter. Now drag your mouse over different text and the format will instantly change. Like you painted it on!
Home	Font	**Font Choice** — Calibri (Body)		The font name here shows the font you are using. Click on the little arrow to see the many fonts available. You can use the scroll bar on the right side of the list to see more fonts. Slide your mouse over and click on any font to choose it. You can change the style of font in a document at any time.
Home	Font	**Font Size**	11	This shows what point size your font is. This font is size 12, this is 14. Click on the little arrow and you'll see a list of font size options. You can change the font size to almost any size you want. You can also click your cursor in the box and type a number for the font size right there!

27

The Tour Guide

TAB	GROUP	COMMAND	ICON	USE
Home	Font	**Grow Font**	A˄ A˅	Highlight some text and click on the larger "A" to grow the font 2 sizes at a time.
Home	Font	**Shrink Font**	A˄ A˅	Highlight some text and click on the smaller "A" to shrink the font 2 sizes at a time.
Home	Font	**Change Case**	Aa ▾	This is handy to bulk change the case of typed work. Change to: lowercase, UPPERCASE, Sentence case, Capitalize Each Word or tOGGLE cASE.
Home	Font	**Clear Formatting**		Highlight text and click on this to remove all special formatting, leaving only plain, regular text.
Home	Font	**Bold Text**	**B**	Click on this to change your text to **bold text**. Or, highlight the **bold text** and click on this to change it back to regular text.
Home	Font	**Italic Text**	*I*	Click on this to change text from regular to *italic*. Click on it again to go back to regular.
Home	Font	**Underline**	U̲	Click on this to <u>underline your text</u>. Click on the tool again to remove the underline formatting. Highlight text to underline in bulk. Click on the little arrow beside it to see different underline styles!
Home	Font	**Strike-through**	a̶b̶c̶	Use this tool to draw a line through text, making it look like it's ~~crossed~~ out.

28

The Tour Guide

TAB	GROUP	COMMAND	ICON	USE
Home	Font	**Subscript**	x₂	Click on *Subscript* and you can create type that is smaller and just below the line, like ₜₕᵢₛ.
Home	Font	**Superscript**	x²	Click on *Superscript* and you can create type that is smaller and just above the line, like ᵗʰⁱˢ.
Home	Font	**Text Effects**	A	Click on this and change your text into **art-like** letters with fancy outlines or glowing shadows! Click on the little arrow to see all your options.
Home	Font	**Highlight Text**	ab✏ ▾	Drag your mouse over text and click on this to make it look like you've dragged a highlight marker over the text. Click on the little arrow to choose different colors.
Home	Font	**Text Color**	A ▾	Click on this to choose different colors for your typing. You can change any text to any color, anytime you want.
Home	Paragraph	**Bullet List**	≔	• This is a bullet list. • Click on the Bullet List icon. • Now, when you hit the return key a bullet will show at the start of every line. • Click on it again to turn off the bullet list formatting. • Click on the little arrow for more style options.

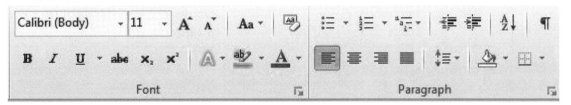

29

The Tour Guide

TAB	GROUP	COMMAND	ICON	USE
Home	Paragraph	**Numbered List**		1. This is a numbered list. 2. When you click on this, then hit the return key, a number will appear for the next line. 3. Click on the little arrow for more style options. 4. Click on it again to turn it off.

Home	Paragraph	**Multi-level List**		• Use this to create multi-level lists.
				  • Like this, with
				    • some lines further
				    • indented within the list.

Home	Paragraph	**Indent Left**		Highlight text and click on this to move all the text over to the next "tab" position going left. Often it moves about a half-inch at a time.
Home	Paragraph	**Indent Right**		Highlight text and click on this to move all the text over to the next "tab" position going right. Often it's about a half-inch at a time.
Home	Paragraph	**Sort**		Fabulous tool! Highlight text then click on this tool to sort lists or paragraphs alphabetically or numerically.
Home	Paragraph	**Show/Hide Format Markers**		Documents are laced with hidden formatting code markers. Most of the time you don't want to see the hidden markers, but if you do, click on this tool to show or hide them!

30

The Tour Guide

TAB	GROUP	COMMAND	ICON	USE
Home	Paragraph	**Align Text Left**		Align the text to the left margin of your document. You can align by paragraph or the whole document.
Home	Paragraph	**Center Text**		Align your text in the center, between both the right and left margins. You can align by paragraph or the whole document.
Home	Paragraph	**Align Text Right**		Align text to the right margin of your document. You can align by paragraph or the whole document.
Home	Paragraph	**Justify Text**		Justified text means that your text will be stretched out to meet each edge of the margins. Most novels have justified text.
Home	Paragraph	**Line and Paragraph Spacing**		Click on this to change the spacing that you see between the lines. You can change the spacing between all lines as well as the space you see between paragraphs.
Home	Paragraph	**Shade Painter**		Highlight any text and click on this to bulk highlight an area. Click on the little arrow to see all the colors you can choose!
Home	Paragraph	**Borders**		Use this tool to create boxes around paragraphs or even sentences. Click on the little arrow to see the many styles and colors!

Paragraph

31

The Tour Guide

TAB	GROUP	COMMAND	ICON	USE
Home	Styles	**Formatting Styles**	AaBbCcDdE ¶ Normal	Style Sets are preset formats for documents. Instead of individually setting formats for each line or section, a Style Set will help you keep a nice professional look to a document.
Home	Editing	**Find**	🔍	Click on Find and a window pops open. Type in the word or phrase you're looking for and almost instantly it will point it out for you.
Home	Editing	**Replace**	ab/ac	This tool works with Find. Perhaps you spelled something wrong. Click on Find, type in the misspelled word. e.g., lousie. Click on Replace, type Louise. Choose to change all the errors or replace one at a time.
Home	Editing	**Select**	▷	Click on the little arrow to see your options; Select All, Select Objects... Select what you want then choose your editing option.

The Tour Guide

TAB	GROUP	COMMAND	ICON	USE
Insert	Pages	**Cover Page**		Fabulous tool for creating and placing a cover page on a document. Click on the little arrow to see all the choices!
Insert	Pages	**Insert Blank Page**		Position your cursor somewhere on your document and click on Blank Page; a new blank page will get inserted right there.
Insert	Pages	**Page Break**		Click your cursor exactly at the line where you want your page to end. Then, use this tool to ensure that is exactly where the page will *break* between pages.
Insert	Tables	**Table**		Click on the little arrow to see many options for inserting a table. *After* you insert a table, the ribbon will change to show all the Table tools. See pages 56—59 for more about creating tables.
Insert	Illustrations	**Picture**		Click on this and you'll open a window where you can search for an image file in your computer to put in your document. After you insert a picture, the ribbon will change to show all the Picture Formatting tools. See pages 62—65 for more on inserting pictures.

33

The Tour Guide

TAB	GROUP	COMMAND	ICON	USE
Insert	Illustrations	**Clip Art**		Click on Clip Art and you'll see hundreds of royalty-free pictures and drawings available to you. In the window that opens, type in a word — try *puppy* and see what shows up!
Insert	Illustrations	**Shapes**		Insert an arrow, a thought bubble, a heart... There are lots of choices. Click on the little arrow and see.
Insert	Illustrations	**Smart Art**		Talk about making flow-charts easy! Click on this and see the possibilities.
Insert	Illustrations	**Chart**		This works together with the program Excel. It will help you convert data to a chart on your Word document. (Not *quite* as easy as that though.)
Insert	Illustration	**Screenshot**		Use this tool to insert a picture of any open window on your computer that is not minimized into the taskbar. When you click on Screenshot, you'll see all the open program windows. Click on one of the windows and it will instantly get inserted as a picture in your document. Cool!
Insert	Links	**Hyperlink**		A hyperlink is something that, when clicked on, links to another place. The link can be in the same document or elsewhere. You can link to other text, a picture, e-mail, a website, another document — almost anything!

The Tour Guide

TAB	GROUP	COMMAND	ICON	USE
Insert	Links	**Bookmark**		If you add a bookmark to a location in a document, you can use the Find tool to bring you back to that spot in the future.
Insert	Links	**Cross Reference**		Helpful for large documents. You can create hyperlinks to cross-reference material.
Insert	Header & Footer	**Header**		Headers go at the top of a page, like chapter headings. Click on the little arrow to see different styles.
Insert	Header & Footer	**Footer**		Footers go at the bottom of a page, like page numbers, a design, text... Click on the little arrow to see different styles.
Insert	Header & Footer	**Page Number**		Click on this and easily add page numbers to your document. There are lots of styles to choose from.
Insert	Text	**Text Box**	Text Box ▾	Use this to insert an independent text box on your page. Click on the little arrow to see your options. *I sometimes insert a picture within a text box to give me more flexibility on where the picture can be placed on the page. See page 65 for more about inserting a picture in a text box.*

35

The Tour Guide

TAB	GROUP	COMMAND	ICON	USE
Insert	Text	**Quick Parts**		Quick Parts is a cool tool! Use it to save snippets of things you might have to type over and over. Like your address!
Insert	Text	**Word Art**		Word Art is great for creating artsy looking text on posters or covers. Highlight some text and click on this to see all the cool styles and options!
Insert	Text	**Drop Cap**		Drop Cap formatting; that is what it is called when you see the first letter or few words in a paragraph very large and then the rest of the printing is normal.
Insert	Text	**Signature Line**		This is for creating a digital signature. With the help of passwords, digital signatures allow you to control who sees your work and what they can do with it.
Insert	Text	**Date & Time**		Click on this and you'll see a dozen or more options for showing date and time. Click on any of them to insert it into your document.
Insert	Text	**Object**		Click on this if you want to insert another document into your current document.

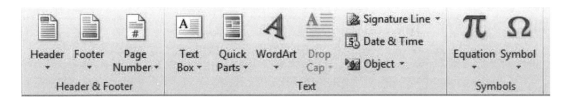

36

The Tour Guide

TAB	GROUP	COMMAND	ICON	USE
Insert	Symbols	**Equation**	π	If you are a math teacher or algebra nut, this is the tool for you. With this tool you can insert many pre-defined math equations.
Insert	Symbols	**Symbol**	Ω	From hieroglyphics to happy faces, arrows to British pound signs, you'll find them all here!
Page Layout	Themes	**Themes**	Aa	Themes and Styles are similar. Microsoft explains the difference this way, "Imagine that themes are a well-tailored suit for your document. Styles are the various shirts and ties you can match with the suit to make it your own."
Page Layout	Themes	**Colors, Fonts and Effects**		For a consistent look to a document, use these tools to help you customize the colors and fonts used.
Page Layout	Page Setup	**Margins**		You guessed it. This is where you can set up the margins on your page. Click on the little arrow to see the endless options. You can change your margins over and over again.
Page Layout	Page Setup	**Orientation**		Portrait or Landscape. Portrait is set up like a regular letter. Landscape is a regular letter on its side.

37

The Tour Guide

TAB	GROUP	COMMAND	ICON	USE
Page Layout	Page Setup	**Size**		Most documents will be Letter size. With the Size tool you can choose whatever size you want for the end product — index cards, envelopes, custom sizes, whatever!
Page Layout	Page Setup	**Columns**		Highlight your typing, then click on the Columns tool to convert the typing into columns. Great for creating a brochure or newsletter!
Page Layout	Page Setup	**Breaks**		Insert different types of "breaks": a page break, a column break, a break in the middle of a line...
Page Layout	Page Setup	**Line Numbers**		Sometime you may need to number the lines in a document. This will do just that for you.
Page Layout	Page Setup	**Hyphen-ation**		With this tool you can get Word to insert hyphens automatically, tell it not to hyphenate, or tell it you want to add hyphens manually.
Page Layout	Page Background	**Watermark**		A Watermark is a faded image or text that is placed behind the regular text on the document.
Page Layout	Page Background	**Page Color**		This is good to use for a document that is only going to be seen on a computer. It would use a lot of color in your printer if you printed a whole page with a solid color background!

38

The Tour Guide

TAB	GROUP	COMMAND	ICON	USE
Page Layout	Page Background	**Page Borders**		Click on this to open a window where you'll see lots of nice page border designs to choose from. Really nice touch for a special letter!
Page Layout	Paragraph	**Indent**		Use this tool to specially indent a line, paragraph or section of a document. You can indent from the left or the right margins.
Page Layout	Paragraph	**Spacing**		Use this tool to change the spacing between paragraphs. This does not change the space between lines within a paragraph, where the words and sentences automatically move to the next line (word wrap).
Page Layout	Arrange	**Position object among text**		Use this to position an image or textbox. It can align an object in the middle of your document, at the top, the bottom, the left, the right...
Page Layout	Arrange	**Wrap Text around object**		This is fun to experiment with! Insert a picture onto a document, then click on it—so it is *selected.* Now click on this tool and try out all the options. The text can move around the picture, go over or under it... Try it out and see!

39

The Tour Guide

TAB	GROUP	COMMAND	ICON	USE
Page Layout	Arrange	**Bring Forward & Send Backward**		Imagine you have placed pictures on top of each other. Think of each picture as a layer. With this tool you can move a picture from one layer to another. Bringing Forward or Sending Backward.
Page Layout	Arrange	**Selection Pane**		When you click on this you'll open a little side-bar window that will list all the objects and items that you have put on your page.
Page Layout	Arrange	**Align object**		Click on this to see the tools to help you align objects (like pictures) left, right or centered.
Page Layout	Arrange	**Group Objects**		Hold down the Ctrl or the Shift key and click on various shapes you have drawn, or pictures you've placed on your document to select them. Then, click on this tool to *group* them together as one unit. Click on this tool again to un-group them.
Page Layout	Arrange	**Rotate**		Click on a text box or image, then click on this to open a tool so you can rotate the text box or image around on its axis.

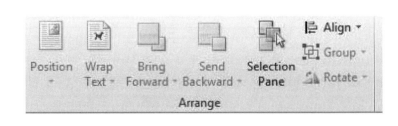

Don't let your pictures jump around on your page; arrange them.

40

The Tour Guide

TAB	GROUP	COMMAND	ICON	USE
References	Table of Contents	**Table of Contents**		The T.O.C. tool looks for headings in your document, then uses those headings to create at T.O.C. Click on the little arrow to see other options or to create different styles.
References	Table of Contents	**Add Text to T.O.C.**		Use this tool to add text, a little indented, to your T.O.C.
References	Table of Contents	**Update T.O.C.**		There is often lots of editing when doing up a T.O.C. This will let you update a small section of it or the whole thing.
References	Footnotes	**Footnote, Insert**	AB^1	Talk about an easy way to insert a footnote! Click your cursor to where you want a footnote[1] and a little number will show up like that, as well as its reference at the bottom (foot) of the page!
References	Footnotes	**Endnote, Insert**		Endnotes are like footnotes, but the reference to the number will be at the end of the document, instead of at the bottom of the page.
References	Footnotes	**Footnote, Next**	AB^1	Use this tool to scroll through the footnotes in your document. Scroll to the Next or the Previous notes.
References	Footnotes	**Show Footnotes**		Click on this and you'll be zoomed to whatever page or pages that footnotes are on.

41

The Tour Guide

TAB	GROUP	COMMAND	ICON	USE
References	Citations & Bibliography	**Insert Citation**		All the tools in this group make inserting citations and adding a bibliography a snap. When you click on Insert Citation a window will open where you can add all the relevant information.
References	Citations & Bibliography	**Manage Sources, Citations**		This is a quick and easy way to edit and manage any sources you quoted in your citations.
References	Citations & Bibliography	**Citation Style**		Highlight a citation and then click on this tool to see how the citation can be displayed differently within your document.
References	Citations & Bibliography	**Biblio-graphy**		All the tools in this group make inserting Citations and adding a Bibliography a snap. The Bibliography tool works with the Citation tool. When you click on Bibliography, almost instantly you'll see it created!
References	Captions	**Caption, Insert**		Use this tool to create a caption above or below a picture, table or graph within a document.
References	Captions	**Caption, Insert Table of Figures**		A Table of Figures is a Table of Contents, but only for the Captions!
References	Captions	**Cross-Reference**		Use this tool to cross-reference words or objects in your document. It creates a hyperlink between the items!

The Tour Guide

TAB	GROUP	COMMAND	ICON	USE
References	Index	**Mark Entry, Index**		This is truly the easiest program to create an index with! Just click your mouse on something you want included in your index then click on this tool and add the entry. When you are done, use the Insert Index tool.
References	Index	**Index, Insert**		When you have finished with Mark Entry, move your cursor to the end of your document and click on this to insert the index!
References	Index	**Index, Update**		Use this tool to update the index at any time.
References	Table of Authorities	**Mark Citation**		Use this tool to help you create a Table of Authorities
References	Table of Authorities	**Table of Authorities**		A Table of Authorities is used on legal documents. It's an index of all the citations you have marked.

Bright Ideas...

_____

_____

_____

— _____

_____

_____

The Tour Guide

TAB	GROUP	COMMAND	ICON	USE
	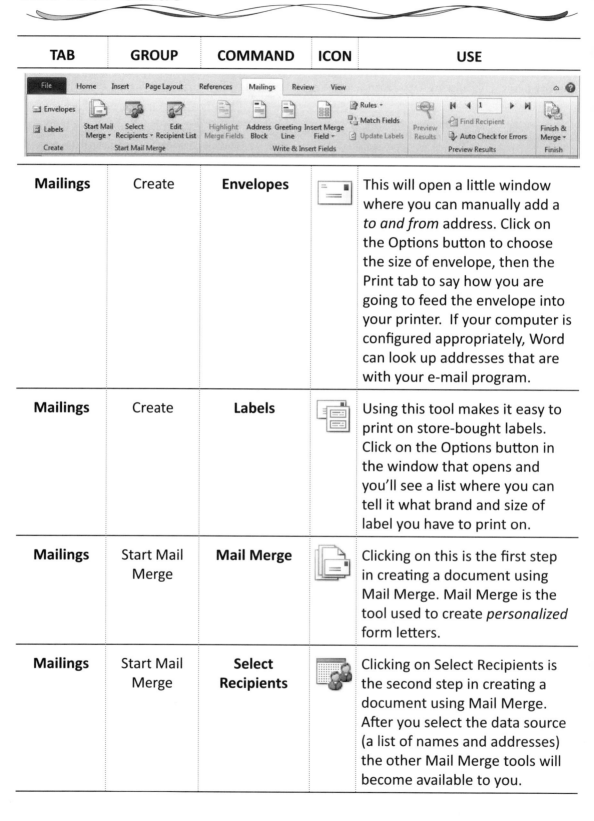
Mailings	Create	**Envelopes**		This will open a little window where you can manually add a *to and from* address. Click on the Options button to choose the size of envelope, then the Print tab to say how you are going to feed the envelope into your printer. If your computer is configured appropriately, Word can look up addresses that are with your e-mail program.
Mailings	Create	**Labels**		Using this tool makes it easy to print on store-bought labels. Click on the Options button in the window that opens and you'll see a list where you can tell it what brand and size of label you have to print on.
Mailings	Start Mail Merge	**Mail Merge**		Clicking on this is the first step in creating a document using Mail Merge. Mail Merge is the tool used to create *personalized* form letters.
Mailings	Start Mail Merge	**Select Recipients**		Clicking on Select Recipients is the second step in creating a document using Mail Merge. After you select the data source (a list of names and addresses) the other Mail Merge tools will become available to you.

The Tour Guide

TAB	GROUP	COMMAND	ICON	USE
Mailings	Start Mail Merge	**Edit Recipient List**		In the data source window that opens, you can tick all the recipients you want to include; un-tick those you don't.
Mailings	Write & Insert Fields	**Merge, Highlight Fields**		When you insert a "Field" it looks like this on your document: <<First>>, what the field is for, surrounded by << >> marks. If you've used a lot of fields in a letter, use this tool to help you spot them! <<Greeting Line>>
Mailings	Write & Insert Fields	**Merge, Address Block**		How formal or informal do you want your letter to be? With the tools found here you can set things up so it uses just the first name, like Joe, or more formal, Mr. Smith, when Mail Merge inserts their address on a letter.
Mailings	Write & Insert Fields	**Merge, Greeting Line**		Would you like your letter to say "Dear" or "To" before the recipient's name? Choose the *greeting line field* you want here.
Mailings	Write & Insert Fields	**Merge, Insert Merge Field**		This is where you will see all the different types of fields you can use. Some are: First Name, Last Name, Home City, Business Name, Phone Number.
Mailings	Write & Insert Fields	**Merge, Rules**		Maybe you want to send out a letter to everyone in your list except the Smyths. With this tool you can create a rule to "skip" the Smyths when it's creating all the merged letters.

The Tour Guide

TAB	GROUP	COMMAND	ICON	USE
Mailings	Write & Insert Fields	**Merge, Match Fields**		Perhaps the titles in the header row of your data source don't match the title options in Merge. You can fiddle things a bit here to make it work.
Mailings	Write and Insert Fields	**Merge, Update Fields**		If you have used the Match Fields tool, use this to update all the Fields that are set in your document.
Mailings	Preview Results	**Merge, Preview Results**		Click on this once to see how your letter will look when it's printed out; click on it again to see the fields.
Mailings	Preview Results	**Merge, Find Recipient**		Maybe you've got 20 people on your list and you would like to see how the letter looks to the 5th person on the list? Use this!
Mailings	Preview Results	**Merge, Auto Check for Errors**		Love this... Auto Check simulates the merge, before you actually have to complete the merge. Saves having to start again if you've messed something up.
Mailings	Finish	**Merge, Finish & Merge**		When you are sure you have everything right, click on Finish. Once you click on Finish, you cannot edit or fix the merge anymore.

46

The Tour Guide

TAB	GROUP	COMMAND	ICON	USE
Review	Proofing	**Spelling & Grammar**	ABC ✓	I lvoe — oops, love spell check! When you sepll something wrong, you'll see it underlined in red. Click on Spelling & Grammar to check all or just a selected part of a document. In the Spell Check window that opens, you can choose to change, add or ignore incorrectly spelled words that it finds.
Review	Proofing	**Research**		Highlight a word or term in your document, then click on this tool to open a sidebar with internet search engine results for that word or phrase. Pretty cool stuff!
Review	Proofing	**Thesaurus**		This is SO much more than just a plain old thesaurus. Highlight a word and click on Thesaurus to see all your options. Click on the little arrow near the top to see all the places it can look words up in; even in other languages! You have to be connected to the internet to take advantage of all the language tools.
Review	Proofing	**Word Count**	ABC 123	Click on this and you'll not only see how many words are in your document, but also how many characters, spaces, paragraphs, lines...

47

The Tour Guide

Tip:
Customize your dictionary!
File > Options > Proofing > Custom Dictionaries
or, Auto Correct Options!

Do your fingers make the same typing mistakes over and over again? You can use auto-correct and you won't have to worry about it anymore.

1. Open the Auto Correct window.

2. In the box below where it says Replace, type how you usually mis-type the word.

3. Put a tick in the little spot beside "With" and everything will to come to life!

4. Type the correct spelling for the word in the box directly below "With".

5. Click on "ADD" and you've done it.

6. Click on OK to exit the window!

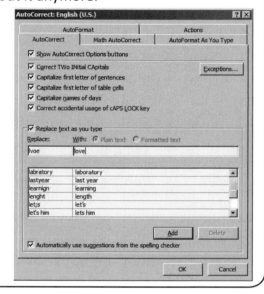

Bright Ideas...

___
___
___
___
___
___
___
___

The Tour Guide

TAB	GROUP	COMMAND	ICON	USE
Review	Language	**Translate**		Fabulous tool! Click on Translate and have a look at the various options. You can translate a word, a phrase or a block of text. Try it out, it's fun to do. You have to be connected to the internet to use this tool.
Review	Language	**Language**		This opens the same window that you'll find by clicking through File>Options>Language. It's where you set the default language you want to work in.
Review	Comments	**Comment: New, Delete, Previous & Next**		If you are working on a document with other people, using Comments is a great way for everyone to put in their two cents worth.
				Comments look either like sticky notes or can be in line with the document. They do not become part of the original document until you "Accept" them.
				◊ Place your cursor where you want to position a comment and click on New Comment to create a new comment.
				◊ Click on a Comment then click on the Delete Comment icon to delete it.
				◊ Use the Previous and Next icons to scroll through comments in a document.

49

The Tour Guide

TAB	GROUP	COMMAND	ICON	USE
Review	Tracking	**Track Changes**		Track Changes is good if other people are actually editing your document, not just commenting on it. Click on the icon to see it change from grayed out to active-looking. Now, click your cursor somewhere in your document and type something. The new typing will show up in red. Delete something and you'll see it crossed out. You will see everything you change, add or edit. Use the Accept or Reject Changes tools to accept or reject any changes you make!
Review	Tracking	**Tracking: Final**		Use this to **stop seeing** all the Tracking Comments and Markups. Click on the little arrow beside the icon to see four options. *FINAL and ORIGINAL will give you a cleaned-up, regular view.*
Review	Tracking	**Tracking: Show Markup**		Click on *Show Markup* to see the different ways edits and comments can be shown.
Review	Tracking	**Tracking: Reviewing Pane**		Click on *Reviewing Pane* and choose to see the markups beside or below the main body of work.
Review	Changes	**Tracking: Accept Changes**		This works in tune with Track Changes. If you like a change that was made, click on this to accept it.

50

The Tour Guide

TAB	GROUP	COMMAND	ICON	USE
Review	Changes	**Tracking: Reject Changes**		This works in tune with Track Changes. If you do not like a change that was made, click on this to reject it!
Review	Changes	**Tracking Changes: Previous, Next**		Use these tools to scroll through changes made in a document.
Review	Compare	**Compare**		Use this to compare two documents and display what has been changed between them. The comparison is referred to as a legal blackline.
Review	Protect	**Block Authors**		This tool is available only if you are sharing the document on a compatible internet workspace. It will let you block areas of your document so other people can't change or edit it.
Review	Protect	**Restrict Editing**		Set up a document password here so only people who know the password can work on it.

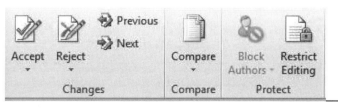

"By golly, you've created a whole new skill set here!"

51

The Tour Guide

TAB	GROUP	COMMAND	ICON	USE
View	Document Views	**Print Layout**		This is the view most people like to see. It shows how your document would look printed out on paper.
View	Document Views	**Full Screen Reading**		Click on this and you won't see the ribbon! The document and background will fill the window. Look way over to the right side at the top and click on CLOSE to go back to the regular view.
View	Document Views	**Web Layout**		Documents don't always look the same when they are posted on a website. Use this tool to help you out with that.
View	Document Views	**Outline**		This is a good view to use if things aren't looking right and you can't figure out why. Click on Outline to see all the hidden characters or other funky things hiding in your document...
View	Document Views	**Draft**		In Draft view, you won't see any headers, footers, images or graphs. All you'll see is the text in the main body. It's a good view to use when editing a long multi-part document.

The Tour Guide

TAB	GROUP	COMMAND	ICON	USE
View	Show	**Ruler**	☐ Rul ☐ Gri ☐ Nav	Click on Ruler to see or not see rulers at the edges of the document window. To change to a different type of measurement, click through this path: File > Options > Advanced > Display. Then you can choose inches, centimeters, millimeters, picas or points.
View	Show	**Gridlines**	☐ Rul ☐ Gric ☐ Nav	Click on Gridlines and your "paper" will look like graph paper. It's a great tool for laying out designs!
View	Show	**Navigation Pane**	☐ Rulɛ ☐ Gric ☐ Nav	Super tool for searching through a document! Click on it and you'll open a sidebar with three tabs. Navigate through headings, pages, even by words or phrases! Tick or un-tick the box to see the Navigation Pane.
View	Zoom	**Zoom**	🔍	*Zoom!* Zoom in/zoom out. From seeing your document at only 10% of its size to 500% of its size. The Zoom tools are a great help if you are visually impaired. If you've got the zoom slider visible at the bottom of the window, it does the same things.

53

The Tour Guide

TAB	GROUP	COMMAND	ICON	USE
View	Window	**New Window**	New Window	When you click on this you will open a copy of the document you are working on in a completely new window. It's a handy tool if you want to see what different editing looks like on one and then compare it to the original.
View	Window	**Arrange All**	Arrange All	If you have more than one document open at a time you can use this tool to view them all at once on your desktop.
View	Window	**Split**	Split	Maybe you want to zoom in and work on a special effect in your document, but also want to see how the document looks as a whole with the changes. With this tool you can do that! View your document in two different views at the same time.
View	Window	**Switch Windows**	Switch Windows	If you have multiple windows and/or documents open at one time you can click on this tool to switch between them.
View	Windows	**Macros**	Macros	A macro is a tiny program you can create with the developer tools found under the Developer tab. Developing macros are way beyond the purpose of this book, so that's all I'm saying about them here. If you would like to learn more about developing Macros, click on Help. *Microsoft's Office Help Page* is a good place to start.

54

Bright Ideas

That's it for the Tour Guide!

I hope you had fun and feel confident to try things out on your own now.

On the next few pages, learn more about working with tables and inserting pictures.

Go Wild!

Working with Tables

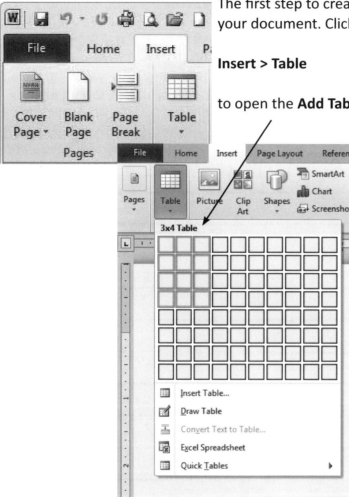

The first step to creating a table is to **Insert** it into your document. Click through:

Insert > Table

to open the **Add Table menu**.

Without pressing down either click, slide your mouse over the number of squares that you want your table to be. The squares highlight as your mouse slides over them!

In Table terms, each square is called a Cell.

Here I've slid over 3 columns wide and 4 rows high.
See where it says "3x4 Table".

When the squares you've highlighted are the number of rows and columns that you want, left-click to insert the table in your document.

Now that you have a table in your document, you can:

◊ Adjust the size of table.
◊ Adjust the width of the columns.
◊ Adjust the height of the rows.
◊ Change the style of the table.
◊ Change the style of the lines.
◊ Merge cells together.
◊ Split cells in two, or three or…
◊ Add more rows or columns or delete them.

Now that the table is set, the possibilities are endless!

Working with Tables

Now you see it... Now you don't... That's the case with the *Table Tools tabs*. When you click on, and are working with a table, the Table Tools tabs, *Design* and *Layout* show up. When you are not working on the table, you don't see them.

If you don't see the Table Tools tabs, click on the table to activate them!

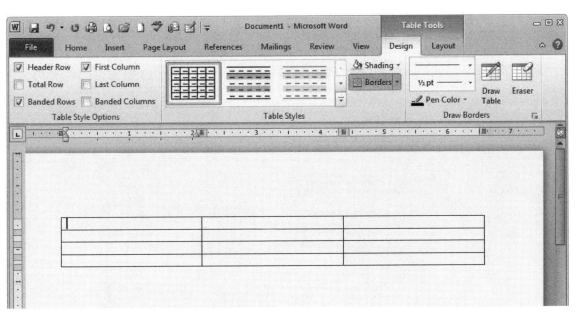

Here's how to manually re-size columns and rows.

You can drag-and-drop lines to move them!

1. Slide your mouse over a line in your table that you would like to move.

2. Your cursor will turn into a little double line with arrows when you are right over the line. (Kind of like I show here.)

3. When you see this little double arrow straddling the line, hold down the left click on your mouse.

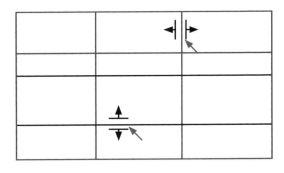

4. With the mouse click held down, slide the cursor to move the lines!

5. Let go of the mouse click when the line is where you want it.

You can't move the borders on the very left and on the top; they anchor your table.

Working with Tables

You can manually re-size a table or, use the Table Properties window!

There are two ways to open the Table Properties window.

1. If you right-click when your cursor is in a cell, you will open a mouse menu with lots of Table Tools in it, including Table Properties. Move your cursor and left-click on Table Properties to open its window.

2. You can also click on the Table Properties command in the Ribbon. Find it here: Table Tools > Layout tab > Table Properties (On the left side in the Table Group.)

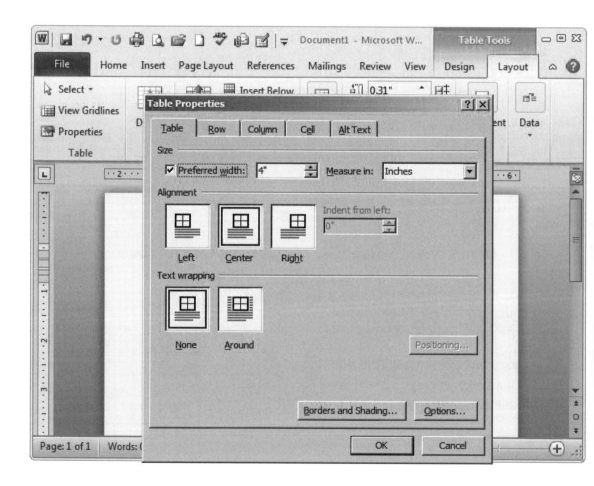

Tick the little box beside where it says *Preferred width* to be able to type in a measurement in the other box beside it. Here I typed in 4.

When I click on the OK button, at the bottom of the window, I'll go back to see my table all re-sized to 4" wide!

Working with Tables

Open the Table Properties window again and let's have a quick look around. Notice that there are five tabs on the Table Properties window. Click on each one to see what's under them. You'll see that you can set specific heights and widths for columns and rows. You'll see that you can set the alignment for each cell—whether the typing in the cells is aligned on the bottom, to the top or centered. Lots of good info here...

Most of the tools you find in the Properties window are also under the *Table Tools* tabs.

Creating great tables is not hard, but it does take some practice. The best way to go about it, is to create a table just to practice on. Try out the tools and see what they do!

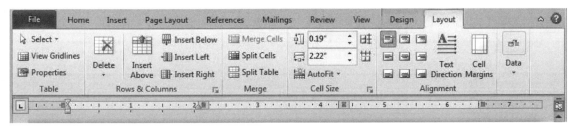

Highlight the table and:

- ◊ Click on the different Styles shown under the Design tab. See all the looks!
- ◊ Type in a few cells and click on different Alignments under the Layout tab.
- ◊ Click your cursor into a cell and click on *Insert Above* under the Layout tab to insert a row above the cell you are in.
- ◊ Try out the Shading tool.
- ◊ To delete a table, row or column, click on Delete under the Layout tab.

Experiment, and you will discover great things!

Tips:

Click your cursor into any cell, then **use the tab or arrow keys** on your keyboard to move to the next cell. This is a MUCH easier way to quickly move from one cell to the next.

You can sort a whole table alphabetically! Highlight the table, then click on Data under the Layout tab. Click on the A/Z icon to see your sorting options!

Bright Ideas

Bright Ideas

Inserting a Picture

Here's how to insert Clip Art onto a document:
It's easier to learn by doing, so let's practice with the *Row Your Boat* file.

1. Open the file we created earlier, Row Row Your Boat.

2. Click through Insert > Clip Art
   ◊ The Clip Art window will open.

3. Type 'row boat' in the Clip Art search window, then click on *Go* to do the search.
   ◊ If you are on the internet, tick the box beside where it says *Include Office.com content* to let Word search online too.
   ◊ LOTS of clip art images will appear in the window below. Scroll through and pick one you like.

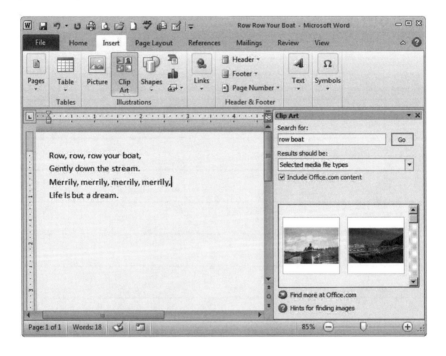

You can drag & drop a picture onto your document or, just click on it.
Don't worry about how a picture lands on your page.
Once an image is there you can move it, change its size… Edit like crazy!

Here's how to *drag and drop* an image.

1. Hold your left-click down over the image.

2. While holding the left-click down, drag the picture over to your document. Let go of the left-click and drop the picture when it's there!

Inserting a Picture

If you like, you can close the clip art window by clicking on its X.

> DO YOU HAVE LIVE PREVIEW ENABLED? With Live Preview enabled, you will be able to see how an image changes when you slide your mouse over different picture formatting tools. Find Live Preview: File > Options > General.

The Picture Tools tab is a *"now you see it, now you don't"* tab. It only shows up when you have clicked on a picture, telling Word you want to do something with it. If you don't see *Picture Tools*, click on a picture to activate it, then click the *Format tab* to see the tools.

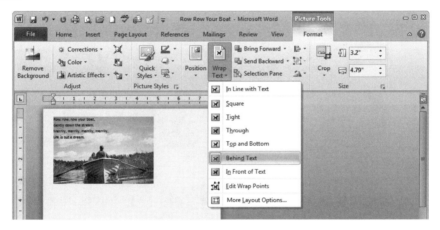

C*hoose how you want to lay out your picture with position and wrap text.*

◊ You can move your picture to where you want it by clicking on Position and choosing an option.
◊ Click on *Wrap Text* and try out the options to see how the picture can work with your text.

Try out different formatting tools. If you have Live Preview enabled, you will see the picture get re-formatted when you slide over each command. It's a pretty cool feature!

When you click on a picture, you will see a frame around it with little circles on the corners and midway spots.

Re-Size a picture by holding your left click down over one of these circles and move your mouse. Wider, taller, bigger, smaller...

Move a picture manually by holding down your left-click and moving your mouse when you see this ⇔ appear.

63

Inserting a Picture

Here's how to insert a picture that you have saved in your computer:

1. Click Insert > Picture, to open the Pictures folder in your Library.

2. Click on the picture you want, then on the Insert button to place it on your document. You can also double click on a picture to insert it.

Here's how to look for and find pictures in your computer:

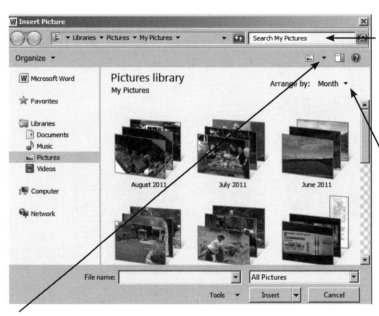

If you have previously given a picture a name, you can find it by typing its name in the *Search My Pictures* window, or by typing its name in the *File name* box.

Here, my pictures are arranged by Month. You have to click on a *month* (May, June...) to open a folder and see its contents.

Click on the little arrow to see other ways of arranging your folders.

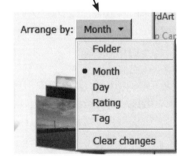

You can view your files in different ways.
Here, I am looking my files by *Large Icons*. Click on the little arrow that I'm pointing to above, to open this menu where you can use the slider to see other views.

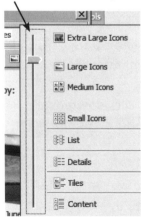

Try the different views out on your computer to see how your files can be displayed.

Tip
You can also use the Search window that is part of the Start menu to search for pictures. The Search window in the Start menu searches all over your computer, not just in one folder at a time.

64

Inserting a Picture

Customize where a picture is placed on your document.
The trick is to place the picture inside a text box! A text box can be moved anywhere.
Here's how:

First, create the Text Box.

◊ Click through: Insert > Text Box.

◊ Choose a simple text box. The text box will land somewhere on your document. It might already have text in it that you'll have to delete.

◊ *You can move and resize a text box any time, before or after you put a picture in it.*

  ◊ Move a text box by moving your mouse inside the box. When you see this, hold down the left-click and move your mouse.

  ◊ Re-size a text box by holding down your left-click over any of the edge markers and slide your mouse.

Second, place a picture in the text box.

◊ Click your mouse inside the text box. (This is important to do.)

◊ Then click through: Insert > Picture, and search for the picture or clip art you want.

  ◊ When you click on a picture to insert it, it will land directly in the text box.

  ◊ Click on the picture in the Text Box and the *Picture Tools Format ribbon* will show up.

Third, format the lines on the text box.

◊ Click on the text box so you see the little circle markers around the edge of it.

◊ When you select the text box, the *Drawing Tools Format ribbon* shows up.

◊ Click on *Shape Outline*, in the *Shape Styles* group.

◊ Choose a color, style or no outline at all!

Between the *Picture Tools ribbon* and the *Drawing Tools ribbon* there is a lot you can do with pictures. Experiment with everything here. Don't be afraid to try things out.

After all, the best way to learn is to do!

Bright Ideas

The Command Index

Now that you've done The Tour Guide and know your way around, you will enjoy having The Command Index at hand.

*You'll never lose commands or tools again!
Finding them is a snap with The Command Index.*

Find all the tools and commands in alphabetical order.

Here's how it works:

1. *Find the COMMAND you want, listed alphabetically.*
2. *Click on the TAB that's referenced beside it.*
3. *Look for the GROUP that's referenced beside that.*
4. *Find the COMMAND you want.*

It's a snap!

The Command Index

COMMAND	TAB	GROUP	ICON	USE
Add Text to T.O.C.	References	Table of Contents		Use this tool to add text, a little indented, to your T.O.C.
Align object	Page Layout	Arrange		Click on this to see the tools to help you align objects (like pictures) left, right or centered.
Align Text Left	Home	Paragraph		Align the text to the left margin of your document. You can align by paragraph or the whole document.
Align Text Right	Home	Paragraph		Align text to the right margin of your document. You can align by paragraph or the whole document.
Arrange All	View	Window	Arrange All	If you have more than one document open at a time, you can use this tool to view them all at once on your desktop.
Bibliography	References	Citations & Bibliography		All the tools in this group make inserting Citations and adding a Bibliography a snap. The Bibliography tool works with the Citation tool. When you click on Bibliography, almost instantly you'll see it created!
Block Authors	Review	Protect		This tool is available only if you are sharing the document on a compatible internet workspace. It will let you block areas of your document so other people can't change or edit it.

68

The Command Index

COMMAND	TAB	GROUP	ICON	USE
Bold text	Home	Font	**B**	Click on this to change your text to **bold text**. Or, highlight the **bold text** and click on this to change it back to regular text.
Bookmark	Insert	Links		If you add a bookmark to a location in a document, you can use the Find tool to bring you back to that spot in the future.
Borders	Home	Paragraph		Use this tool to create boxes around paragraphs or even sentences. Click on the little arrow to see the many styles and colors!
Breaks	Page Layout	Page Setup		Insert different types of "breaks": a page break, a column break, a break in the middle of a line...
Bring Forward & Send Backward	Page Layout	Arrange		Imagine you have placed pictures on top of each other., Think of each picture as a layer. With this tool you can move a picture from one layer to another; forward or backward.
Bullet List	Home	Paragraph		• This is a bullet list. • Click on the Bullet List icon. • Now, when you hit the return key a bullet will show at the start of every line. • Click on it again to turn off the bullet list formatting. • Click on the little arrow for more style options.
Caption, Insert	References	Captions		Use this tool to create a caption above or below a picture, table or graph within a document.

69

The Command Index

COMMAND	TAB	GROUP	ICON	USE
Caption, Insert Table of Figures	References	Captions		A Table of Figures is a Table of Contents, but only for the Captions!
Case, Change	Home	Font	Aa ▾	This is handy to bulk change the case of typed work. Change to: lowercase, UPPERCASE, Sentence case, Capitalize Each Word or tOGGLE cASE.
Center Text	Home	Paragraph		Align your text in the center, between the right and left margins. You can align by paragraph or the whole document.
Chart	Insert	Illustrations		This works together with the program Excel. It will help you convert data to a chart on your Word document. (Not quite as easy as that though.)
Citation, Insert	References	Citations & Bibliography		All the tools in this group make inserting citations and adding a bibliography a snap. When you click on Insert Citation a window will open where you can add all the relevant information.
Citation, Style	References	Citations & Bibliography		Highlight a citation and then click on this tool to see how the citation can be displayed differently within your document.
Clear Formatting	Home	Font		Highlight text and click on this to remove all special formatting, leaving only plain old regular text.

70

The Command Index

COMMAND	TAB	GROUP	ICON	USE
Clip Art	Insert	Illustrations		Click on Clip Art and you'll see hundreds of royalty-free pictures and drawings available to you. In the window that opens, type in a word — try *puppy* and see what shows up!
Close	File		**File > Close** Use the Close command to close a document, but leave Word open. More on closing a document on page 8.
Colors, Fonts and Effects	Page Layout	Themes		For a consistent look to a document, use these tools to help you customize the colors and fonts used.
Columns	Page Layout	Page Setup		Highlight your typing, then click on the Columns tool to convert the typing into columns. Great for creating a brochure or newsletter!

The Command Index

COMMAND	TAB	GROUP	ICON	USE
Comment: New, Delete, Previous & Next	Review	Comments		If you are working on a document with other people, using Comments is a great way for everyone to put in their two cents worth. Comments look either like sticky notes or can be in line with the document. They do not become part of the original document until you "Accept" them. ◊ Place your cursor where you want to position a comment and click on New Comment to create a new comment. ◊ Click on a Comment then click on the Delete Comment icon to delete it. ◊ Use the Previous and Next icons to scroll through comments in a document.
Compare	Review	Compare		Use this to compare two documents and display what has been changed between them. The comparison is referred to as a legal blackline.
Copy	Home	Clipboard		Highlight text or an image then click on Copy to copy it. Then, click your cursor where you want to put it and click on Paste! *Voilà!* The keyboard shortcut for Copy is Ctrl + C

72

The Command Index

COMMAND	TAB	GROUP	ICON	USE
Cover Page	Insert	Pages		Fabulous tool for creating and placing a cover page on a document. Click on the little arrow to see all the choices!
Cross-Reference	Insert	Links		Helpful for large documents. You can create hyperlinks to cross-reference material.
Cross-Reference	References	Captions		Use this tool to cross-reference words or objects in your document. It creates a hyperlink between the items!
Cut	Home	Clipboard		Highlight an image or text, click on Cut and you'll *cut* it out of the document, ready to *Paste* somewhere else.
Date & Time	Insert	Text		Click on this and you'll see a dozen or more options for showing date and time. Click on any of them to insert it into your document.
Draft	View	Document Views		In Draft view, you won't see any headers, footers, images or graphs. All you'll see is the text in the main body. It's a good view to use when editing a long multi-part document.
Drop Cap	Insert	Text		Drop Cap formatting; that is what it is called when you see the first letter or few words in a paragraph very large and then the rest of the printing is normal.

73

The Command Index

COMMAND	TAB	GROUP	ICON	USE
Edit Recipient List	Mailings	Start Mail Merge		In the data source window that opens, you can tick all the recipients you want to include; un-tick those you don't.
Endnote, Insert	References	Footnotes		Endnotes are like footnotes, but the reference to the number will be at the end of the document, instead of at the bottom of the page.
Envelopes	Mailings	Create		This will open a little window where you can manually add a *To* and *From* address. Click on the Options button to choose the size of envelope, then the Print tab to say how you are going to feed the envelope into your printer. If your computer is configured appropriately, Word can look up addresses that are with your e-mail program.
Equation	Insert	Symbols	π	If you are a math teacher or algebra nut, this is the tool for you. With this tool you can insert many pre-defined math equations.
Exit	File	**File > Exit** Click on Exit and you will exit and close Word and the document you are working on. With Word 07, find *Exit Word* on the bottom right corner of the File menu window.		
File tab in Word 2010	The File tab replaced the Office Logo in 2010. Clicking on either opens the File menu.			

74

The Command Index

COMMAND	TAB	GROUP	ICON	USE
Find	Home	Editing		Click on Find and a window pops open. Type in the word or phrase you're looking for and almost instantly Word will point it out for you.
Font Choice	Home	Font Calibri (Body)		The font name here shows the font you are using. Click on the little arrow to see the many fonts available. You can use the scroll bar on the right side of the list to see more fonts. Slide your mouse over and click on any font to choose it. You can change the style of font in a document at any time.
Font Size	Home	Font	11	This shows what point size your font is. This font is size 12, this is 14. Click on the little arrow and you'll see a list of font size options. You can change the font size to almost any size you want. You can also click your cursor in the box and type a number for the font size right there!
Footer	Insert	Header & Footer		Footers go at the bottom of a page, like page numbers, a design, text... Click on the little arrow to see different styles.
Footnote, Insert	References	Footnotes	AB[1]	Talk about an easy way to insert a footnote! Click your cursor to where you want a footnote[1] and a little number will show up like that, as well as its reference at the bottom (foot) of the page!

75

The Command Index

COMMAND	TAB	GROUP	ICON	USE
Footnote, Next	References	Footnotes		Use this tool to scroll through the footnotes in your document. Scroll to the Next or the Previous notes.
Footnotes, Show	References	Footnotes		Click on this and you'll be zoomed to whatever page or pages that footnotes are on.
Format Painter	Home	Clipboard		Highlight a typing format you like then click on the Format Painter. Now drag your mouse over different text and the format will instantly change, like you painted it on!
Formatting Styles	Home	Styles		Style Sets are preset formats for documents. Instead of individually setting formats for each line or section, a Style Set will help you keep a nice, professional look to a document.
Full Screen Reading	View	Document Views		Click on this and you won't see the ribbon! The document and background will fill your whole screen. Look way over to the right side at the top and click on CLOSE to go back to the regular view.
Gridlines	View	Show		Click on Gridlines and your "paper" will look like graph paper. It's a great tool for laying out floor plans!

76

The Command Index

COMMAND	TAB	GROUP	ICON	USE
Group Objects	Page Layout	Arrange		Hold down the Ctrl or the Shift key and click on various shapes you have drawn, or pictures you've placed on your document to select them. Then, click on this tool to *group* them together as one unit. Click on this tool again to ungroup them.
Grow Font	Home	Font	A˄ A˅	Highlight some text and then click on the larger "A" to grow the font 2 sizes at a time.
Header	Insert	Header & Footer		Headers go at the top of a page, like chapter headings. Click on the little arrow to see different styles.
Help	File	**File > Help** Click on the question mark icon to open Microsoft's *online* help pages. If you're not on the internet, Help isn't much help... This is also where you get Word to check for online updates.		
Highlight Text	Home	Font		Drag your mouse over text and click on this to make it look like you've dragged a highlight marker over the text. Click on the little arrow to choose different colors.
Hyperlink	Insert	Links		A hyperlink is something that, when clicked on, links to another place. The link can be in the same document or elsewhere. You can link to other text, a picture, e-mail, a website, another document — almost anything!

77

The Command Index

COMMAND	TAB	GROUP	ICON	USE
Hyphen-ation	Page Layout	Page Setup		With this tool you can get Word to insert hyphens automatically, tell it not to hyphenate, or tell it you want to add hyphens manually.
Indent	Page Layout	Paragraph		Use this tool to specially indent a line, paragraph or section of a document. You can indent from the left or the right margins.
Indent Left	Home	Paragraph		Highlight text and click on this to move all the text over to the next "tab" position going left. Often it moves about a half-inch at a time.
Indent Right	Home	Paragraph		Highlight text and click on this to move all the text over to the next "tab" position going right. Often it's about a half-inch at a time.
Index, Insert	References	Index		When you have finished with the Mark Entry tool, move your cursor to the end of your document and click on this to insert the index!
Index, Update	References	Index		Use this tool to update the index at any time.
Info	File *or in* Word 07 the Office Logo	**File > Info** If you have a document open, when you click on File it will default to opening on Info, showing you basic information about that document. The Info screen covers up the page you are working on. The page you are working on is still there, just behind this window. *Info* is also where you find the tools to set up **Document Protection,** *set up a* **Password** *or prepare it for* **Sharing**.

78

The Command Index

COMMAND	TAB	GROUP	ICON	USE
Insert Blank Page	Insert	Pages		Position your cursor somewhere on your document and click on Blank Page; a new blank page will get inserted right there!
Italic Text	Home	Font	*I*	Click on this to change text from regular to *italic*. Click on it again to go back to regular.
Justify Text	Home	Paragraph		Justified text means that your text will be stretched out to meet each edge of the margins. Most novels have justified text.
Labels	Mailings	Create		Using this tool makes it easy to print on store-bought labels. Click on the Options button in the window that opens and you'll see a list where you can tell it what brand and size of label you have to print on.
Language	Review	Language		This opens the same window that you'll find by clicking through File>Options>Language. It's where you set the default language you want to work in.
Line and Paragraph Spacing	Home	Paragraph		Click on this to change the spacing that you see between the lines. You can change the spacing between word-wrapped lines as-well-as the space you see between paragraphs.
Line Numbers	Page Layout	Page Setup		Sometime you may need to number the lines in a document. This will do just that for you.

79

The Command Index

COMMAND	TAB	GROUP	ICON	USE
Macros	View	Windows	Macros	A macro is a tiny program you can create with the developer tools found under the Developer tab. Developing macros are way beyond the purpose of this book, so that's all I'm saying about them here. If you would like to learn more about developing Macros, Microsoft's Office Help Page is a good place to start.
Mail Merge	Mailings	Start Mail Merge		Clicking on this is the first step in creating a document using Mail Merge. Mail Merge is the tool used to create *personalized* form letters.
Manage Sources: Citations	References	Citations & Bibliography		This is a quick and easy way to edit and manage any sources you quoted in your citations.
Margins	Page Layout	Page Setup		You guessed it. This is where you can set up the margins on your page. Click on the little arrow to see the endless options. You can change your margins over and over again.
Mark Citation	References	Table of Authorities		Use this tool to help you create a Table of Authorities; used in legal documents.
Mark Entry, Index	References	Index		This is truly the easiest program to create an index with! Just click your mouse on something you want included in your index then click on this tool and add the entry. When you are done, use the Insert Index tool.

80

The Command Index

COMMAND	TAB	GROUP	ICON	USE
Merge: Address Block	Mailings	Write & Insert Fields		How formal or informal do you want your letter to be? With the tools found here you can set things up so it uses just the first name, like Joe, or more formal, Mr. Smith, when Mail Merge inserts their address on a letter.
Merge: Auto Check for Errors	Mailings	Preview Results		Love this... Auto Check simulates the merge before you actually have to complete the merge. Saves having to start again if you have messed something up.
Merge: Find Recipient	Mailings	Preview Results		Maybe you've got 20 people on your list and you would like to see how the letter looks to the 5th person on the list? Use this!
Merge: Finish & Merge	Mailings	Finish		When you are sure you have everything right, click on Finish. Once you click on Finish, you cannot edit or fix the merge anymore.
Merge: Greeting Line	Mailings	Write & Insert Fields		Would you like your letter to say "Dear" or "To" before the recipient's name? Choose the *greeting line field* you want here.
Merge: Highlight Fields	Mailings	Write & Insert Fields		When you insert a "Field" it looks like this on your document: <<First>>, what the field is for, surrounded by << >> marks. If you've used a lot of fields in a letter, use this tool to help you spot them! <<Greeting Line>>

The Command Index

COMMAND	TAB	GROUP	ICON	USE
Merge: Insert Merge Field	Mailings	Write & Insert Fields		This is where you will see all the different types of fields you can use. Some are: First Name, Last Name, Home City, Business Name, Phone Number...
Merge: Match Fields	Mailings	Write & Insert Fields		Perhaps the titles in the header row of your data source don't match the title options in Merge. You can fiddle things a bit here to make it work.
Merge: Preview Results	Mailings	Preview Results		Click on this once to see how your letter will look when it's printed out; click on it again to see the fields.
Merge: Rules	Mailings	Write & Insert Fields		Maybe you want to send out a letter to everyone in your list except the Smyths. With this tool you can create a rule to "skip" the Smyths when it's creating all the merged letters.
Merge: Update Fields	Mailings	Write and Insert Fields		If you have used the Match Fields tool, use this to update all the Fields that are set in your document.

Multi-level List	Home	Paragraph		- Use this to create multi-level lists.
				  - Like this, with
				    - some lines further
				      - indented within the list.

The Command Index

COMMAND	TAB	GROUP	ICON	USE
Navigation Pane	View	Show	☐ Rule ☐ Gric ☐ Nav	Great tool for searching through a document! Click on it and you'll open a sidebar with three tabs. Navigate through headings, pages, even by words or phrases! Tick or un-tick a box to see the Navigation Pane.
New	File	**File > New** Click on New to see all the different types of documents Word can create. From a plain blank page to fancy documents like resumes, faxes, cards, agendas, calendars... So many choices!		
New Window	View	Window	New Window	When you click on this you will open a copy of the document you are working on in a completely new window. It's a handy tool if you want to see what different editing looks like on one and then compare it to the original.
Numbered List	Home	Paragraph		1. This is a numbered list. 2. Click on this and when you hit the return key, a number will appear for the next line. 3. Click on the little arrow for more style options. 4. Click on it again to turn it off.
Object	Insert	Text		Click on this if you want to insert another document into your current document.
Office Logo Word 07	The File tab was replaced by the Office Logo in 2010. Clicking on either opens the File menu.			

83

The Command Index

COMMAND	TAB	GROUP	ICON	USE
Open	File	**File > Open** Click through File > Open to open a window where you can search for a saved document. More on opening documents on page 10.		
Options	File	**File > Options** Find the *Options* here to personalize and customize Word. Learn more about these Options starting on page 16.		
Orientation	Page Layout	Page Setup		Portrait or Landscape. Portrait is set up like a regular letter. Landscape is a regular letter on its side.
Outline	View	Document Views		This is a good view to use if things aren't looking right and you can't figure out why. Click on Outline to see all the hidden characters or other funky things hiding in your document...
Page Borders	Page Layout	Page Background		Click on this to open a window where you'll see lots of nice page border designs to choose from. Really nice touch for a special letter!
Page Break	Insert	Pages		Click your cursor exactly at the line where you want your page to end. Then, use this tool to ensure that is exactly where the page will *break* between pages.

84

The Command Index

COMMAND	TAB	GROUP	ICON	USE
Page Color	Page Layout	Page Background		This is good to use for a document that is only going to be seen on a computer. It would use a lot of color in your printer if you printed a whole page with a solid color background!
Page Number	Insert	Header & Footer		Click on this and easily add page numbers to your document. There are lots of styles to choose from.
Paste	Home	Clipboard		Use this to Paste a picture or text *after* you have "copied" it. The keyboard shortcut for Paste is Ctrl + V.
Picture	Insert	Illustrations		Click on this and you'll open a window where you can browse for an image file in your computer to put in your document. After you insert a picture, the ribbon will change to show all the Picture Formatting tools. See pages 62—65 for more info.
Position Object Among Text	Page Layout	Arrange		Use this to position an image or textbox. It can align an object in the middle of your document, at the top, the bottom, the left, the right...
Print	File	**File > Print** Click through this path to open the Print window. To learn more about how to print, go to page 11.		
Print Layout	View	Document Views		Print Layout is the view most people like to see; it shows how your document will look printed out on paper.

85

The Command Index

COMMAND	TAB	GROUP	ICON	USE
Quick Parts	Insert	Text		Quick Parts is a cool tool! Use it to save snippets of things you might have to type over and over; like your address!
Recent	File	\multicolumn{3}{l}{**File > Recent** Click on Recent to see a list of all the saved files you've recently had open, with the most recent at the top of the list. Just slide your mouse over and click on the name of the file you want to open.}
Replace	Home	Editing		This tool works with Find. Perhaps you spelled something wrong. Click on Find, type in the misspelled word. e.g., lousie. Click on Replace, type Louise. Choose to change all the errors or replace one at a time.
Research	Review	Proofing		Highlight a word or term in your document, then click on this tool to open a sidebar with internet search engine results for that word or phrase. Pretty cool stuff!
Restrict Editing	Review	Protect		Set up a document password here so only people who know the password can work on it.
Rotate	Page Layout	Arrange		Click on a text box or image, then click on this to open a tool so you can rotate the text box or image around on its axis.

86

The Command Index

COMMAND	TAB	GROUP	ICON	USE
Ruler	View	Show	☐ Rul ☐ Gri ☐ Na\	Click on Ruler to see or not see rulers at the edges of the document window. To change to a different type of measurement, click through this path: File > Options > Advanced > Display. Then you can choose inches, centimeters, millimeters, picas or points.
Save & Send	File	**File > Save & Send** These tools can help you to save your document in a variety of formats suitable for emailing, posting on a blog, putting on a website or sending to another computer in your network.		
Save or Save As	File	**File > Save** This is where you find the tools to save a document. If you click either Save or Save As, you'll open the Save As window. More on saving documents starting on page 4.		
Screenshot	Insert	Illustration		Use this tool to insert a picture of any open window on your computer that is not minimized into the taskbar. When you click on Screenshot, you'll see all the open program windows. Click on one of the windows and it will instantly get inserted as a picture in your document.
Select	Home	Editing	⌖	Click on the little arrow to see your options; Select All, Select Objects... Select what you want then choose your editing option.

87

The Command Index

COMMAND	TAB	GROUP	ICON	USE
Select Recipients	Mailings	Start Mail Merge		Clicking on Select Recipients is the second step in creating a document using Mail Merge. After you select the data source (a list of names and addresses) the other Mail Merge tools will become available to you.
Selection Pane	Page Layout	Arrange		When you click on this you'll open a little side-bar window that will list all the objects and items that you have put on your page.
Shade Painter	Home	Paragraph		Highlight any text and click on this to bulk highlight an area. Click on the little arrow to see all the colors you can choose!
Shapes	Insert	Illustrations		Insert an arrow, a thought bubble, a heart... There are lots of choices. Click on the little arrow and see.
Show/Hide Format Markers	Home	Paragraph		Documents are laced with hidden formatting code markers. Most of the time you don't want to see the hidden markers, but if you do, click on this tool to show or hide them!
Shrink Font	Home	Font		Highlight some text and click on the smaller "A" to shrink the font 2 sizes at a time.
Signature Line	Insert	Text		This is for creating a digital signature. With the help of passwords, digital signatures allow you to control who sees your work and what they can do with it.

88

The Command Index

COMMAND	TAB	GROUP	ICON	USE
Size	Page Layout	Page Setup		Most documents will be letter size. With the Size tool you can choose whatever size you want for the end product — index cards, envelopes, custom sizes, whatever!
Smart Art	Insert	Illustrations		Talk about making flow-charts easy! Click on this and see the possibilities.
Sort	Home	Paragraph		Fabulous tool. Highlight text then click on this tool to sort lists or paragraphs alphabetically or numerically.
Spacing	Page Layout	Paragraph		Use this tool to change the spacing between paragraphs. This does not change the space between lines within a paragraph, where the words and sentences automatically move to the next line (word wrap).
Spelling & Grammar	Review	Proofing		I lvoe — oops, love spell check! When you sepll something wrong, you'll see it underlined in red. Click on Spelling & Grammar to check all or just a selected part of a document. In the Spell Check window that opens, you can choose to change, add or ignore incorrectly spelled words that it finds. You might want to add your own name to Word's dictionary if it shows up as a spelling mistake!

The Command Index

COMMAND	TAB	GROUP	ICON	USE
Split	View	Window	Split	Maybe you want to zoom in and work on a special effect in your document, but also want to see how the document looks as a whole with the changes. With this tool you can do that! View your document in two different views at the same time.
Strike-through	Home	Font	abc	Use this tool to draw a line through text, making it look like it's crossed out.
Subscript	Home	Font	x_2	Click on *Subscript* and you can create type that is smaller and just below the line, like $_{this}$.
Superscript	Home	Font	x^2	Click on *Superscript* and you can create type that is smaller and just above the line, like ^{this}.
Switch Windows	View	Window	Switch Windows	If you have multiple documents open at one time you can click on this tool to switch between viewing them.
Symbol	Insert	Symbols	Ω	From hieroglyphics to happy faces, arrows to British pound signs—you'll find them all here!
Table	Insert	Tables	Table	Click on the little arrow to see many options for inserting a table. *After* you insert a table, the ribbon will change to show all the Table tools. See pages 56—59 for more about creating tables.
Table of Authorities	References	Table of Authorities		A Table of Authorities is used on legal documents. It's an index of all the citations you have marked.

90

The Command Index

COMMAND	TAB	GROUP	ICON	USE
Table of Contents	References	Table of Contents		The T.O.C. tool looks for headings in your document, then uses those headings to create at T.O.C. Click on the little arrow to see other options or to create different styles.
Text Box	Insert	Text		Use this to insert an independent text box on your page. Click on the little arrow to see your options. *I sometimes insert a picture within a text box to give me more flexibility on where the picture can be placed on a page. See page 65 for more about inserting a picture in a text box.*
Text Color	Home	Font		Click on this to choose different colors for your typing. You can change any text to any color, anytime you want.
Text Effects	Home	Font		Click on this and change your text into *art-like* letters with fancy outlines or glowing shadows! Click on the little arrow to see all your options.
Themes	Page Layout	Themes		Themes and Styles are similar. Microsoft explains the difference this way: *Imagine that themes are a well-tailored suit for your document. Styles are the various shirts and ties you can match with the suit to make it your own.*

The Command Index

COMMAND	TAB	GROUP	ICON	USE
Thesaurus	Review	Proofing		This is SO much more than just a plain old thesaurus. Highlight a word and click on Thesaurus to see all your options. Click on the little arrow near the top to see all the places it can look words up in — even in other languages! You have to be connected to the internet to take advantage of all the language tools.
Track Changes	Review	Tracking		Track Changes is good if other people are actually editing your document, not just commenting on it. Click on the icon to see it change from grayed out to active-looking. Now, click your cursor somewhere in your document and type something. The new typing will show up red. Delete something and you'll see it crossed out. You will see everything you change, add or edit. Use the Accept or Reject Changes tools to accept or reject any changes you make!
Tracking Changes: Previous, Next	Review	Changes		Use these tools to scroll through changes made in a document.
Tracking Changes: Accept	Review	Changes		This works in tune with Track Changes. If you like a change that was made, click on this to accept it.

92

The Command Index

COMMAND	TAB	GROUP	ICON	USE
Tracking Changes: Reject	Review	Changes		This works in tune with Track Changes. If you do not like a change that was made, click on this to reject it!
Tracking: Final	Review	Tracking		Use this to **stop seeing** all the Tracking Comments and Markups. Click on the little arrow beside the icon to see four options. *FINAL and ORIGINAL will give you a cleaned-up, regular view.*
Tracking: Reviewing Pane	Review	Tracking		Click on *Reviewing Pane* and choose to see the markups beside or below the main body of work.
Tracking: Show Markup	Review	Tracking		Click on *Show Markup* to see the different ways edits and comments can be shown.
Translate	Review	Language		Fabulous tool! Click on Translate and have a look at the various options. You can translate a word, a phrase or a block of text. Try it out, it's fun to do. You have to be connected to the internet to use this tool.
Underline	Home	Font	U	Click on this to underline your text. Click on the tool again to remove the underline formatting. Highlight text to underline in bulk. Click on the little arrow beside it to see different underline styles!
Update Table (T.O.C.)	References	Table of Contents		There is often lots of editing when doing up a T.O.C. This will let you update a small section of it or the whole thing.

93

The Command Index

COMMAND	TAB	GROUP	ICON	USE
Watermark	Page Layout	Page Background		A Watermark is a faded image or text that is placed behind the regular text on the document.
Web Layout	View	Document Views		Documents don't always look the same when they are posted on a website. Use this tool to help you out with that.
Word Art	Insert	Text		Word Art is great for creating *artsy* looking text on posters or covers. Highlight some text and click on this to see all the cool styles and options!
Word Count	Review	Proofing		Click on this and you'll not only see how many words are in your document, but also how many characters, spaces, paragraphs, lines...
Wrap Text Around Object	Page Layout	Arrange		This is fun to experiment with! Insert a picture onto a document, then click on it—so it is *selected*. Now click on this tool and try out all the options. The text can move around the picture, go over or under it... Try it out and see!
Zoom	View	Zoom		*Zoom!* Zoom in/zoom out. From seeing your document at only 10% of its size to 500% of its size. The Zoom tools are a great help if you are visually impaired. If you've got the zoom slider visible on the status bar, it does the same things.

Bright Ideas

Great Job!

Bright Ideas

Bright Ideas

My Parents Go Wild for Word

You might be surprised that there is not an index here.
The fact is, the book is too simple to do one up. If you need to learn how to use *Word*,
go to *Get Started* and then follow *The Tour Guide*. If you need to look up a specific tool
or command, you'll find it alphabetically listed in *The Command Index*.
You will find what you need here. Quick and simple!

Get Started	1
The Tour Guide	21
Working with Tables	56
Working with Pictures	62
The Command Index	67

Living, Loving, Learning—always.

www.MyParentsFirst.com

Have a computer question? Email me and I'll do my best to help you out!